UPON A WAILING WISH STARS WONDER

POETRY

ANGELO SPIZZARRI

© 2019 Angelo Spizzarri
ALL RIGHTS RESERVED

www.SPIZZARRI.com

No part of this book may be reproduced or utilized in any form or by any means, electronic or mechanical, including photocopying, recording or by any information storage and retrival system, without the prior written permission of the author.

Book page layout & cover by Spizzarri Entertainment Ltd.

PRINTED IN THE UNITED STATES OF AMERICA
THIS BOOK IS PRINTED ON ACID FREE PAPER

ISBN-13: 978-0-9779731-7-0

All words & Face logo: Angelo Spizzarri
Cover Art: Angelo Spizzarri
Photo: Jason Clay Oneal

DO NOT FAULT
THE MIRROR WHEN
IT REVEALS YOUR
IMPERFECTIONS

CONTENTS

1. AN ANXIETY
2. EXHAUSTED DOUBLE
3. THE RED TEAR
4. SOUL LOVE
5. IN THE SEA
6. A SOUL IS FAR
7. CRYING SECLUSION
8. PHANTOM SEA
9. AFTERWARD
10. TRANSMISSION OF
11. THE STARS
12. MY TEETH HURT
13. IN A HAZE OF FALLING
14. STINGING TONGUE
15. DAWNING IS OVER
16. REBIRTH
17. I CANNOT
18. LIQUID LOVE
19. APHRODISIAC
20. A THOUSAND
21. I PROMISE
22. THIS VESSEL
23. THE PHANTOM WALKS
24. JAGGED ORGASM
25. I BECOME WEAKER
26. BLUE MEMORIES
27. UNKNOWN FEELING
28. REVERSE FEVER
29. FAR AWAY
30. PALE KEEPSAKE
31. FORGOTTEN FEELING
32. YOU ARE FAR AWAY
33. ABORTION OF LOVE
34. LOVE QUARANTINED
35. CRYING COCOON
36. I EAT YOUR
37. I SEVER
38. A CATERPILLAR
39. BEYOND THIS
40. MY FINGERS
41. SUNRISE FURTHER
42. WISH AT THE
43. A FOREVER BURNING
44. SILENT SLEEPING
45. SPECTRAL TASTE
46. NUMB FEVER
47. SEA OF THE
48. PRAYER FOR RAIN
49. HALLUCINATE TRAUMA
50. PRETTIEST
51. MELTING BEAUTY
52. SLEEPWALKING HEART
53. ISOLATING FETUS
54. I'VE CUT MYSELF
55. SEVERAL TEARS
56. A SPECTRE WAS SPLIT
57. LOVE SONG
58. I WOULD CRY
59. SOUL PUMPING
60. DISCONNECTED
61. I REMEMBER
62. FURTHER THE DISTANT
63. I CANNOT RESIST
64. ABSENCE
65. TUNNEL
66. OCEAN
67. PATH
68. WEEPING

CONTENTS CONTINUED

69 STRUGGLE
70 MACHINE
71 THE TEAR AND THE FLAME
72 COLLECTOR
73 WANDERING
74 PROGENTIOR
75 REMORSE
76 SALT
77 DESOLATION
78 MONOLITH
79 AVENGING
80 EDGE
81 BLOODLITE
82 SPECTRE
83 TICK TOCK
84 INNOCENCE
85 THE CRIMSON DISC
86 STARS CRY
87 THE KEEPSAKE
88 THE DRIFTING CLOUDS
89 I GAZE AT
90 THE TATTOO BURNS
91 AS I BREATHE
92 SOARING THROUGH
93 I GAZE OUT
94 I EAT CONSUMED
95 TONIGHT THE STARS
96 SLEEP DOES NOT COME
97 MY HEARTS SONG
98 TWINIGHT
99 I LISTEN TO THE WIND
100 THE MEMORY OF YOU

UPON A WAILING WISH STARS WONDER

POETRY

ANGELO SPIZZARRI

AN ANXIETY
EMBRACES THIS GHOST INSIDE
I WISH IT AWAY

EXHAUSTED DOUBLE
A DOPPLEGÄNGER WITHERS
SLOWLY INTO ITSELF

THE RED TEAR
NOT A JEWEL, CRIED –
FROM MY WOUNDED HEART

SOUL LOVE
BLOOMING AS IF
AN EVENING ANGEL STAR

IN THE SEA
OF CONFUSION
I CANNOT DROWN

A SOUL IS FAR FROM FETUS
I LICK A HOLE INSIDE YOU
A TENDER KISS IS ISOLATION

CRYING SECLUSION
INIVISIBLE TO A WORLD –
WORLD – I AM SORRY…

PHANTOM SEA
SILENCE
PURE CHAOS
WAIT
I AM LOST

AFTERWARD
VIRUS FLICKER
ENDLESS BURN
SILKWORM NEAR
WAILING WALL
WAITS FOREVER

TRANSMISSION OF
PAIN IS QUARANTINE
I AM DISORIENTED
ENDLESS MOON
ENDLESS HEART

THE STARS
ABOVE ME ARE BLIND
IN JAGGED FREEZE FRAME

MY TEETH HURT
BUT I CANNOT
TOUCH THEM
LIKE MY PAIN

IN A HAZE OF FALLING EYES
AFTER DAY HAS DAWNED
BURNING IN THE EVENING CALM
MY NERVE ENDINGS
ARE LIKE LIVE WIRES –
THE SOUL SILENTLY CRIES

STINGING TONGUE
FALLING SYNDROME
EATING LUST
EATING EVERYTHING
CICADA IS WHISPERING

DAWNING IS OVER
SECLUSION
I BELONG TO YOU
LOVE SONG
QUIET AND
SECLUDED STAR
THE ASPHYXIA
IS WAITING

REBIRTH
FATED TO BE SO
TRANSPARENT THORN
A PURE SCAR CONSTELLATION
WITHIN A BOTTOMLESS
WEEPING SEA

I CANNOT
SURRENDER FEAR
WITHOUT SCREAMING
THE LAST DAYS LIGHT
LIQUID SNOW FALLING
GHOST TWINS
A TENDER KISS

LIQUID LOVE
MORNING STAR MEMORIES
ATMOSPHERE IS DRINKING
DISINTEGRATION
I EAT YOUR INFECTED
RIPPLING BLOOD VESSEL

APHRODISIAC
TEARDROP
AND TEETH
INFINITE WOMB
WAXING AND WANING
INSIDE A PURE
WAVELENGTH

A THOUSAND
BLACK HEARTS
RAIN FOREVER
THIS BURNING
IS INTOXICATING
I AM DYING

I PROMISE
WHERE AS THIS
FEELING
DISAPPEARED TO
YOU ARE GONE
I STILL LOVE YOU
FOREVER
I PROMISE

THIS VESSEL
IS FORGOTTEN
THIS HEART MOANS
I FEEL A VACUUM
MY SENSES SEVER
A FLOATING DISGUISE
MY SENSES REMAIN

THE PHANTOM WALKS
ALONE WITH MY HEART
TOGETHER
NEAR THE EDGE
OF THE SEA

THE PHANTOM
SENSES FEEL
MY HEART IS NUMB
AN AGITATION STAINS
THE OXYGEN AIR

A FLOATING
VACUUM VIOLENCE
MY SENSES MELTING
FEELING PALE
THE EMERGENCE
HAS GONE

JAGGED ORGASM
IS SCREAMING
A GHOST KISSING A STAR
REBIRTH IS BLISS
I MISS YOU

I BECOME WEAKER
A DISCONNECTED CELL
A DISTURBANCE
A KEEPSAKE
MELTING WITHIN A HAZE
A PHEONIX IS BURNING

BLUE MEMORIES
WANTING A RESURRECTION
BLOSSOMING A FETUS
LICKING A THOUGHT
SALIVA SEEPING OUT

UNKNOWN FEELING
UNPREDICABLE
BRUISED
EXHAUSTED
NOTHING CAN TAKE THIS
LOVE OUT ME

REVERSE FEVER
WITHIN DARK MATTER
THIS HEAVY TORTURE
A KISS A SADNESS
PRAYING MANTIS
DOES NOT CRY AT
WAILING WALL

FAR AWAY
A GHOST REMEMBERED
ITSELF ALONE
DOUBLE CORONA
ECLIPSED A SUN
BEFORE MY EYES
SEPARATION
NOTHING FEELS
REJUVENATED STARS
ARE SICK TONIGHT

PALE KEEPSAKE
YOU ARE STILL
INFECTED
WHERE HAS THIS
PARALYSED
FEELING GONE
LETHARGIC HAZE

FORGOTTEN FEELING
FROZEN ON A WAVE
OF SLIPSTREAM
ECLIPSED BY AN
EMPTY NUMBING
THAT PENETRATES
THIS STATE OF SOUL

ARTERY
EXHAUSTED
TO THE POINT
OF WASTING
INTO OXYGEN
MY EYES CANNOT SEE
THIS HEART IS IN PAUSE
A QUIET ZONE
A QUIET ZONE

FORGOTTEN WORLD
IS CRYING
A TRANSPARENT
TEARDROP
IS LIQUID
DISINTEGRATION
TOMORROW
IS WHISPERING
YOU ARE FAR AWAY

ABORTION OF LOVE
IS NEEDED
EXTREME VIRUS
OF SORROW
IS BITING
BUTTERFLY
OF THE MOON
IS FORGOTTEN

LOVE
QUARANTINED
DESIRE IS
BOTTOMLESS
A THOUSAND
OPAL WAVES
UPON A WISH
UNFOLDS REALITY
A RED REBIRTH
IS UNSTABLE
SOLITUDE –
I AM FULL

CRYING
COCOON
I LOVE YOU
I PIERCE MY
HEAVY HEART
TOGETHER
ENDLESSLY
A THOUSAND
RED SCARS
BURNING
FALLING
DENSITY
INSIDE
I AM LOST

I EAT YOUR
MELTING KISS
MY PARALYSED HEART
IS SLIPPING AWAY
FROM THIS
IRRITATED SOUL
THIS SEPARATION
IS EUPHORIA

I SEVER
MY SENSES
THIS NERVOUS
FEVER IS HIDDEN
MY GOD IS
SYMPHATHY

A CATERPILLAR SLEEPING
UPON A LIQUID DAWN
CONSCIOUSNESS RISING
IN A COLD AFTERGLOW
TRANQUILITY RIPPLING
INSIDE A REFLECTING
DOUBLE ZENITH
MY SADNESS IS PURE

BEYOND THIS
TENDER KISS
TRAUMA TORTURES
MY TEETH
DISINTEGRATION
WEEPING A
BOTTOMLESS SEA

MY FINGERS
DIPPING INSIDE
MY SENSES
BLEACHED
SALIVA CHOKING
I BECOME WEAKER
THIS CONSTRANT
IS ANXIOUS

SUNRISE
FURTHER
HURTS MY
REJECTED EDEN
I CRAVE A HAZE
WITHIN FEAR
LIQUID SKY DIES

WISH AT THE
EDGE OF A SEA
WANTING
ANAESTHETIC
THIS UNREST
IS IMPOSSIBLE
THIS HEART
IS WORRIED

A FOREVER BURNING
CONFUSION RECOGNISED
MY DROWNING DISGUISE
ENLIGHTMENT WITHOUT
A SOUL MATE
THIS FALLEN ANGEL
INSIDE CHAOS

SILENT SLEEPING
CONVULSION
THIS FATAL FLESH
IS THIRSTY
THE CRESCENT MOON
IS IN SLOW MOTION
TONIGHT

SPECTRAL
TASTE OF THE
SCREAMING
ORGASM
BLOOMING A
LETHARGIC FEAR
PERVERSE SALIVA
DIGUISED AS CHAOS
DISSOLVING AND
UNPREDICTABLE
THIS FLESH IS
HEAVY AT TIMES
TOMORROW
IS NOT HERE

NUMB
FEVER IS RISING
TO BOILING POINT
CAN'T FLY
WITHOUT WINGS
WEAKNESS TURNS
INTENSE
THE HEAT HAS
STOLEN AWAY
THE COLD

SEA OF THE
SHOOTING STAR
EYE IS SILENCE
WEEPING RESURRECTION
UNSTABLE KISS OF SADNESS
EVOLVING IN MOURNING
FEARING SOMETHING
IT CANNOT SEE
ZERO DEGREE
FOREVER

PRAYER FOR RAIN
NEVER RECEIVED
A THOUSAND
TRANSPARENT
TEARDROPS
FROM ONE EYE
ONE EYE CRIES
THE OTHER
ONE LAUGHS
ONLY EYE KNOW
WHICH ONE
IS WHICH
BUT THEY DO
LOOK THE SAME –
DON'T THEY...?

HALLUCINATE TRAUMA
MY SWOLLEN TONGUE
SEARCHING FOR THE SALT
OF YOUR TEARS
ON THE HORIZON
AND THE APPARITION
IS NOT THERE
ANYMORE

PRETTIEST
STAGGERING FLESH
WHERE HAVE YOU GONE TO
IN ATMOSPHERE
I CANNOT TASTE YOU
BRUISED I BECOME RELAXED
SLEEPING CHROMOZONE
CRASHING I SWALLOW YOU
IN A FATAL TWILIGHT
IN MY DREAM
WHICH WILL END

MELTING BEAUTY
DRIPPING INTO MY MOUTH
AFTERTASTE OF
PAIN AND SORROW
STINGS MY TONGUE
SUN HAS SLIPPED AWAY
STARS ARE CRYING
TONIGHT

SLEEPWALKING HEART
SEARCHING FOR LIFEBLOOD
AGITATED VIRUS
EATING AT MY TIRED
BEATING ORGAN
WIND WHISPERING
I KNOW WHAT ITS LIKE
TO BE SAD

ISOLATING FETUS
I AM SORRY
BRILLIANT SNOW FALLING
BEGINNING TO DIE
IN SCREAMING SILENCE
IT CANNOT CRY
SENSES CLONED AND SEVERED
QUIET SNOW STILL FLOATING
ANGUISHED YOU ARE
ALWAYS IN MY HEART

I'VE CUT MYSELF
I'VE DAMAGED MY DISEASE
THE SADNESS HAS
STAINED THIS CLOTH
THE EDGE IS BURNT
ICICLES GROW LONG
IN THE NIGHT
ALONE WITH ME
THEY GROW LONGER
THE MORE I WATCH THEM
SO DOES MY SADNESS

SEVERAL TEARS
HAVE FLOWN BY
LIKE YEARS
AT LEAST I STILL HAVE
THE TASTE OF MY TEARS
TO KEEP ME FROM
MY LONELINESS

A SPECTRE WAS SPLIT
LIKE GEMINI TWIN
THE NEGATIVE SIDE
WENT AWAY TO VOID
THE POSITIVE SIDE WAS
LEFT TO STAY
A FEELING OF
INCOMPLETENESS
GROWS LIKE
UNIVERSE

LOVE SONG
IN THE RISING SUN
A THOUSAND
LIGHT YEARS AWAY
A TRILLION
MOMENTS
FOR SOUL
TO BE WITH
SELF ALONE

I WOULD CRY
INTO THE
BOTTOMLESS
THAN TO
FEEL YOUR
DISTURBANCE
HEAVY AS
DRINKING
THE COLD
SHARP SEA

SOUL PUMPING
OBTAINED EUPHORIA
INTO ITSELF
SEEING AND FEELING
NOTHING
DESIRING
NEGATED DESIRE
SADLY PERVERSE
THIS SOULS LAST DAY

DISCONNECTED
SLIPPING INTO
THE PALE SUN
I FEAR THIS
CRAVING WITHIN
THAT IS ALWAYS
IN MY HEART

I REMEMBER
A DAWN RISING
CONFUSION
HAD GONE AWAY
SEEING WITHIN THIS
DOUBLE NOVA
I WAS NOT ALONE

FURTHER
THE DISTANT SUN
DID NOT BURN
MY COLD EYES
BUT LEFT AN
OZONE AFTERGLOW
THAT PEELED
ILLUSION AWAY

I CANNOT RESIST
MY ANXIETY
REMAINS

ABSCENCE

HUMANOID STANDS STILL
IN A TIME WITHOUT DUST
WRAPPED IN BANDAGES
TO HEAL WOUNDS OF MANY
SELF INFLICTED OTHERS
YEARS AND TEARS FOUGHT
AND LOST IN THE WARS MIST
EYES ARE BLINDED BY AN
ABSENCE OF GOD SIGHT CAN'T
RETURN UNLESS A HEART CAN
OPEN ITSELF BUT THE SWORD
IN THE RIGHT HAND IS DULL IT
CAN'T SLICE OPEN BANDAGES
THAT BIND THE FLESH IT CAN'T
REACH THE HEART WHICH WEARS
THE CROWN OF THORNS THAT
PUNISH INSTEAD OF HEAL IN BLISS

TUNNEL

HORSE WALKS DOWN A TUNNEL
OF TIME SHIFT MOTH WINGS OUT
STRETCHED REVEALING EYES OF
CAMOUFLAGE AND NEAR WAS ITS
MIND A BODY OF VEINS ARTERY
NAKED BRAIN ITS HEAD DANCED
AND MOVED LIKE DREAM MISTS
WITH WINGED HORSE THROUGH
EXISTENCE A TUNNEL WENT ON
ITS MIND STARTED BREAKING DOWN
WALKING LEGS BECAME INJURED
VEINED BODY LIMPING DANCING
HALTED NOW NEEDED SOME HELP
HORSE KNEW IT COULDN'T FINISH
WITHOUT ITS MIND AND ALLOWED HIM
TO RIDE UPON ITS BACK IN TIMESHIFT
FOR NOW TOGETHER THEY WOULD
FIND A WAY OUT FOR THE BODY CAN
LEAD A WAY AND GIVE ITS MIND REST

OCEAN

ON SANDS OF OCEAN IN THE
MOMENTS OF PAST HOURS
GOD SAW THE WATER MOVING
IN WAVES OF TIME WHERE A
BLUE OCTOPUS CAME TO THE
SURFACE FROM DEPTHS TO ASK
A QUESTION TO ITS MAKER
"WHY WAS MAN CREATED LAST
BUT ALSO WHY DOES HE HAVE
THE MOST MENTAL EMOTIONAL
FLAWS?" WINDS BLEW CIRCLING
THE VAST PORTION OF SEA
A LONE BLACK BIRD SWOOPED
IN AND WITH BLINK VANISHED
THEN CAME THE SIMPLE ANSWER
THE OCTOPUS SOUGHT
"WE NEEDED SOMETHING FLAWED
TO BALANCE OUT THE PERFECT
LOGIC THAT CAME TO BE."
SEEMING SATISFIED WITH THIS
THE CREATURE RETURNED TO THE
SAFE CONFINES OF THE DEEP SEA

PATH

SPIRITUALLY DEVINE SITTING IN THE
SKY ON LOTUS LEAF BUDDHA WAS
PERFECTION EYES CLOSED BUT CAN
SEE AND FEEL ALL FOR EYES WERE
NOT NEEDED AS CONSCIOUSNESS
OPEN RADIATING VIBRATIONS OF
TELEPHATIC SPEAKING LANGUAGE
SOARING UP HIGH HE CAME DOWN
TO EARTH LEVEL AND FOUND A CHILD
BORN HUNGRY EMPTY LAYING NEAR
A FRUIT TREE AND AFTER CONVERSING
WITH IT FOR A MOMENT BUDDHA KNEW
IT COULD NOT GIVE IT WHAT IT NEEDED
CHILD WAS IN NEED OF SUSTENANCE
AND LOVE OF FLESH BUT ITS PURE
LIFEFORCE WAS VIBRANT STRONG AND
BUDDHA KNEW HE COULD NEVER MAKE
FOR THIS CHILD THE CHOICE OF ITS
RIGHT OR WRONG PATH IN ITS LIFE

WEEPING

AN ISLAND SITS SILENT IN THE
MIDDLE OF A MIST ACID POND
ON THE EDGE OF THE DISTANT
METEORITE UPON THIS ISLAND
SAT A WEEPING WILLOW TREE
WHOSE BRANCHES MOVED LIKE
BIRD SONG IN THE FAINT BREEZE
THE SUN SET SHONE IN GOLD
AND WHITE JADE SKY AND IT HAD
A WISH IN ITS SLOW ETERNITY TO
HAVE A FRIEND FOR IT WAS DEEPLY
SAD EXISTING HERE ALONE CHRONOS
SLIPPED ON THE EROSION FROM ACID
EATING THE SOIL OF ITS ONLY PLACE
ITS EVER KNOWN WOULD NOT STOP
YET IT STILL WEEPS SILENTLY FOR A
FRIEND SOMEONE TO SHARE ITS LIFE
WITH EVEN IF ITS LIFE WON'T LAST
IT IS AFTER ALL JUST A WISH
AFTER CHRONOS DRIPPED ON
IT WAS GONE AND UNIVERSE
ALTHOUGH COLD SLID ON

STRUGGLE

COLD AND COARSE WERE LAVA ROCKS
BLACK AND CHARRED THAT LITTERED
THE LAND WHERE THE DE – HYDRATED
ONE ROAMED FOR A TIME THEN LOW
HE FOUND A WATERFALL SURGING LIFE
FLUID FILTERING THE BLOOD ORANGE
LIGHT FROM A DISTANT SUN LIKE LAVA
SURROUNDING BARRIER BARBWIRE SO
NO ONE WOULD CROSS IT BUT THIRST
WAS TOO GREAT AND SKIN DRIED TOO
THIN HE THEN ON AUTO BEGAN TO
CRAWL STRUGGLE THROUGH THE WIRE
THAT CUT PRICKED SLICED FRAIL FLESH
TOO DRY AND HURT HANDS CLUTCHING
AND GRASPING FOR THE PRECIOUS
WATER THAT COULD GIVE HIM FILL HIM
WITH LIFE SUSTENANCE TO SURVIVE
AND WITH NO HELP FIGHTING HIMSELF
THE STRUGGLE WAS INTENSE AND REAL

MACHINE

BARREN CONCRETE FLATLAND AN
EMPTY NANO – SPACE DULL AND
LIFELESS IN THIS PLACE SITS A
MACHINE THAT CAN SEPARATE
DEFECTS NEGATED FROM FLESH
AND MIND AS QUIVERING HUMAN
CELL FORMED AN UPRIGHT STANDING
FIGURE INJECTOR INSERTED BLOOD
INTO CERTRIFUGE AND SPINNING
IN 360 DEGREE HUMAN CELL WATCHES
AS PLASMA IS REMOVED MIND THOUGHTS
DESIRES STARTED THE PROCEEDURE
TO SPLICE BUT PANIC BEGAN BEATING
WITHIN DESIRE BEGAN TO SEPARATE IN
FRAGMENTS BUT HUMAN CELLS MIND
SUDDENLY COULD NOT WAIT IT OUT
IT WANTED THE PROCESS FINISHED
NOW IN THIS FUSED IN FEAR SPACE

THE TEAR AND THE FLAME

ONCE UPON A CHRONOS THERE
LIVED THE TEAR AND THE FLAME
WITHIN THE ABYSS OF THOSE WHO
EXIST FOR PLEASURE OR PAIN
WHEN THE FLAME WAS INSIDE THE
EMOTION CELL THE TEAR MISSED
THE FLAME FOR AS TIME SLID BY
THE TEAR DEVELOPED AN ATTRACTION
OF UNKNOWN ORIGIN AND WHILE THIS
WAS TRUE THE TEAR DIDN'T KNOW
THE FLAME HAS SUCCUMBED TO THE
VERY SAME DESIRE FOR THE TEAR
WHEN ONE MOMENT CAME AND NIETHER
WERE INSIDE THE EMOTION CELL THEY
BOTH UNKNOWN TO EACH OTHER WERE
GOING TO GET TOGETHER FOR THE
ATTRACTION WAS BORDERLINE FATAL
THEN STARING INTO EACH OTHERS
ESSENCE THEY CAME TOGETHER AND
THE IMPACT DISINTEGRATED THEM BOTH
CANCELING EACH OTHERS' LIFE FORCE
COMPLETELY OUT OF DIMENSION
THE ABYSS NOW WAS SLIGHTLY EMPTY
JUST FOR THIS CHRONOS

COLLECTOR

IN THE LAND OF ERASED HIGH WITHIN
THE SPHERES OF CORONA CLINGING TO
AN OLD DETERIORATING GOLD GREEN
CIRCUIT BOARD COLLECTOR SAT ATTACHED
AS USED UP OLD MEMORIES PAST OVER
HEAD LIKE MISTS OF SIGHS IN THE MODE
OF CONSUMATION COLLECTOR ATE OF
THESE USED AND USELESS MEMORIES
FOR HE NEVER HAD ANY OF HIS OWN
AND FELT A DEEP LONELINESS WITHIN
ITS CONSCIOUSNESS SO IT SWALLOWED
MORE AND MORE BUT IT WAS AS IF HE WAS
ALWAYS HUNGRY AND MORE WAS SOON
ALL COLLECTOR COULD FEEL AS SPACE
MOVED HE BEGAN TO STIFFEN UP SLOWLY
AT FIRST AND THEN MORE QUICKLY UNTIL
PARALYSIS BEGAN TO SEIZE COLLECTORS
FUNCTIONS MEMORIES FLEW OVER HEAD
THE SPHERES HIS CIRCUITRY STOPPED
ALL HE COULD DO WAS WATCH ALL THAT
HE YEARNED FOR AND WANTED FLY PAST
HIM AND THE ACHE THAT HE WOULD
NEVER EVER HAVE ANY MORE AGAIN
WAS HIS EVER AFTER DEATH

WANDERING

INSIDE THE MAZE OF WANDERING IN THE
AGE OF SAGITTA ROAMED A CATAPILLAR
WHO LIKE MANY OTHERS LET HIS LIFE
CARRY HIM WHERE LIFE WANTED CAUSE
HAD NO DIRECTION BUT WHAT CATAPILLAR
HAD WAS TIME OH LOTS AND LOTS OF TIME
AND AFTER WANDERING AROUND HE CAME
TO A SECTION OF MAZE THAT WAS DEAD
ENDED STANDING FEW HUNDRED FEET TALL
WAS AN IMMENSE HOUR GLASS INSIDE
RAN THE DUST OF TIME AND CATAPILLAR
EXAMINED THE OBJECT ALL OVER BUT JUST
COULDN'T UNDERSTAND JUST WHAT THIS
WAS FOR CATAPILLAR WAS DRUNK ON
ITS OWN SELF – DECEPTION AND THERE
WAS ALWAYS TIME TO DO ANYTHING AND
SITTING THERE THE DUST HAD EMPTIED
A LITTLE BIT AND HIS GLAZED EYES WOULD
NEVER REACH CHRYSALIS NEVER KNOW
THE OTHER FUTURE IT COULD HAVE FELT
AND LIVED AND THE DUST OF ITS OWN LIFE
WOULD RUN AND RUN DOWN UNTIL IT WAS
TOO LATE TO DO ANYTHING AT ALL

PROGENTIOR

BLACK FINE POWDER ASHES SWIRLED AND FLOATED SLOW IN THE WIND THUNDER ROLLED IN THE AFAR A PLANETOID ACTING AS SATALITE GLOW FALLS TO A SPOT AND THEN MUSCULAR WHITE HAND RISES UP NAKED BODY OF MAN ASCENT COMPLETED PROGENITOR AWARE OF SELF GAZED AROUND FOR SOMEONE ELSE SOMETHING GREATER THAN HIM BUT FELT NONE CAUSE CHEMICALS IN HIS MIND MATTER WAS CAUSING EMOTIONAL DAMAGE CONFUSION EATING MEMORY AND ANY GLIMPSE OF AN ABSOLUTE BECAME DEFORMED FROM THIS DEFECTIVE MIND PROGENITOR WAS CREATED BUT CREATED FLAWED BUT THIS WAS NOT HIS FAULT BUT IT WAS HIS SPLINTER IN HIS MIND DRIVING HIM TO SEARCH FOR SOMETHING ELSE TO FILL THIS VOID TIGHTENING INSIDE THE CHEST NOTICING THE BLACK ASH AROUND HIM FROM WHICH HE ROSE WOULD SURELY GIVE THE ANSWER GRABBING A HANDFUL THE MUSCULAR PROGENITOR FROZE ONLY FOR AN INSTANT AND SNORTED SOME UP HIS NOSE THEN SOON HIS MOUTH BORE ALL LARGE SQUARE TEETH VEINS PUMPED AND HIS EYES WENT FROM WHITE TO DARK

REMORSE

A BEING SATURATED BY ITS OWN
REMORSE ENTERS A CATATONIC
STATE SLOWLY OVER CHRONOS
BRAIN STEM BEING IS SOON
RENDERED INCAPABLE OF FEAR
THEN BEING FEELS THE PAIN
IN HIS HANDS AND SPINE AS
IF PARASITE MOVES WITHIN HOST
THEN HOT LONG STEEL BLADES
BURST FROM SKIN AND RAZORS
SNEAK OUT FROM EACH FINGER
ONE AFTER OTHER COPPER ODOR
COAGULATING ON FLESH AND FLOOR
SHIVERING AND SHAKING
WITH ORGASM RENDER BREATHING
IS NOW ALIVE TRANSFORMED
PSYCHOPATHY IS ACHIEVED

SALT

WHITE SANDS STRETCHED FOR
ENTERNITY GENTLE BLUE WAVES
CASCADED IN FROM HORIZON
BIRD CALLS SOLILOQUIES SONATA
ECHOED DOWN FROM 3 – DIMENSIONAL
SKY SEA BREEZES GLIDING CLOUDS
SOLID STATUE OF SALT STOOD
IN SILENCE NEAR THE WATERS EDGE
HER MANY FEATURES AND FACE WERE
WORN AWAY SALTY WINDS HAD ERASED
THEM EONS AGO BUT NO ONE
KNEW OF HER LIVING BEATING HEART
INSIDE THIS CHEST AND THE WAR
WITH HERSELF AND EGO FOR SHE
COULD FEEL THE EMOTIONS AS
COLLISIONS AND CHAOS BECAME
CONFLICT AND TIME SWEPT BY WITH
THE OCEANS WAVES SANDS AND WINDS

DESOLATION

WITHIN THE RUINS OF THE
SILENT MIND THE REMANENTS OF
A CITY NOW DESTROYED BY THE
WAR OF THE THOUGHT WAVES
LAID DUST DEBRIS HAZING OUT
A BRIGHT NEURON SUN WHERE
PSYCHE WAS WANDERING A WISH
TATTERED AND TORN FROM
AFTERMATH OF CIVILIZATION
THERE WERE FEW SCATTERED
LIKE JIGSAW PIECES BARELY
SURVIVING SUSTENCE AND
SHELTER WERE MAKESHIFT
HUDDLING TOGETHER FOR
WARMTH FROM THE COLD
WHERE MEMORIES ALTHOUGH
FRACTURED WERE SHARED
OF A BEAUTIFUL PAST WHERE
THOUGHTS WERE LIVING IN
PEACE AND HARMONY UNTIL
CAME THE DESTRUCTOR
SCHIZOPHERINA

MONOLITH

SHE EXISTED IN
A LIQUID DREAM
WHERE IT WAS
SHE STARING INTO
THE BLACK MONOLITH
WHERE EVEN LIGHT WAS
ABSENT AND SHE WAS
TO GAZE INTO IT
NEVER BEING ABLE TO
FEEL ANYTHING OR
SEE THE BEAUTY
MOVING AROUND FOR
DEEP IN HER HEART SHE
NEVER FELT GOOD ENOUGH
FOR ANYTHING THAT WAS
HEALTHY OR REWARDING
SHE COULD SLIGHTLY
REMEMBER A PAST
LIFE BEFORE THE
MONOLITH IT SEEMED
ALL HAZY BUT NOW
THE DARK MONOLITH
WAS ALL SHE KNEW
AND ALSO
LOVED IT MORE
THAN HERSELF

AVENGING

FROM CLOUDS UP
ON THE HIGHEST
STOOD THE CHERUBIM
AND SERAPHIM SECTS
OF ANGELS ALL WERE
AWAITING ORDERS TO
CARRY OUT AND WAGE
THE NEXT WAVE OF
THE LARGEST ATTACK
THAT WAS NEEDED AS
THERE WAS NO OTHER WAY
THEY COULD REACH THESE
BEINGS THEY WERE SENT
TO OVERSEE BUT THEY HAD IT
ALL WRONG THE LAST AMBUSHES
WERE FUTILE SO ANOTHER
WAY WAS SOUGHT TO BE
CARRIED OUT TO THE
MASSES THE AVENGING WAR
NOW WOULD ATTACK
AND CHARGE THEIR WRAITH
UPON A STATE OF THE MIND
CALLED MUTATION

EDGE

IN A LAND OF SEA CLOUD AND MISTS AN
ANGEL WALKS ALONG AN EDGE WHERE
NIRVANA AND THE MATERIAL PLANE MEET
AN OLD MAN WATCHES HER WANDERING
DANCING STEPS SO FRAIL AND SHAKING
THE HUNCHED ONE WALKED OVER TO
THE WINGED ONE AND WANTED HER
TO TAKE THESE SINS FROM HIM AND
SHOWED THE ANGEL A SATCHEL OF
RANDOM SIZED ROCKS WHICH WEIGHED
DOWN HIS WEAK ARMS FOR HE CARRIED
THESE WITH HIM ALL HIS HUNGRY LIFE
THESE SINS EXHAUSTED HIS BEING AND
THEN THE SOFT LOVING GAZE BEAMED
FULL OF COMPASSION FOR HIM FROM HER
AND TOLD HIM THE SINS YOU CARRIED
HAVE SHOWN THAT YOU ARE READY
TO GIVE UP THE PAST AND CONTINUE TO
THE NEW FUTURE YOU JUST NEED TO
PUT THEM DOWN WHEN YOU ARE READY
THE MAN PAUSED GLANCED AT HER EYES
HIS HEART STOPPED FELL TO THE GROUND
SUNLIGHT SHONE WARM AS THE ANGEL
DANCED WALTZED AWAY ON THE EDGE

BLOODLITE

RED CLOUDS ABOVE MOVED
IN SMOKE BLOTTING OUT THE
WHITE ORB BELOW HUMAN FINGERS
ROSE UP FROM BROKEN SLATE FLAT
LAND MASSIVE FRANTICALLY JERKING
IN MIND SICK WHERE CAME SOFT SPINE
THAT SEARCHED FOR ITS BRAIN
SEPARATION AT BIRTH BECAME ACHE
PAINS SO ROAMING CRACKED ROCK
WITH WARM AIR SOFT SPINE CAME TO
A RECTANGULAR GLASS SARCOPHAGUS
CONTAINING THE LIVING BREATHING
AMPUTATED BRAIN SLICED IN 5 ISOLATED
PARTS THE 5 IMPRISONED SENSES OF
SOFT SPINE THAT WERE MISSING THAT
CAUSED NUMBNESS NOT ALIEN TO HIM
AFTER CHRONOS SUDDENLY REALIZING
THAT THERE WAS NO WAY HE COULD FREE
HIS COUNTERPART A WOUND IN GHOST
SADNESS OPENED HIS SEARCH ENDED
STILL RED CLOUDS CHURNED ABOVE
WARM WINDS CHRONOS SLID SILENTLY ON

SPECTRE

A MOMENT FORGOTTEN IN CHRONOS
SLIPSTREAM WRITHING IN RAINBOW
BEAMS OF LIGHT THE SPECTRE FOUND
HIMSELF WANDERING AS HE SEEMED
TO BE ALWAYS WANDERING THE HOLES
IN HIS ANTI – MATTER SHOWING THE SCARS
AND TEARS IF HIS PAST LIVES AND YES
HE WAS EXHAUSTED AND YES HE YEARNED
FOR THIS PERIOD OF LIFE WOULD COME
TO A HALT AND BE CARRIED BY A NEW
DEATH STATE TO THE NEXT LIFE BUT
THIS WAS NOT BY HIS CONTROL THE
FACULTIES OF THE FUNCTIONS HEREIN
WERE THE ONES THAT KNEW WHEN THIS
SLICE IN CHRONOS WOULD TAKE OCCUR
THE SPECTRE TRIED TO REMEMBER THE
QUASI – PAST WHICH WAS FAR GONE BUT
COULD ONLY HOLD ONTO FRAGMENTS LOST
LIKE FLICKERING REFLECTION OF WHITE
DWARF STAR IN THE INFINTE DISTANCE
LONELY AFRAID HE EXISTED HERE
FOR HE WOULD NOT KNOW THE LIMIT
WOULD NOT KNOW WHAT THAT NEXT
DEATH STATE WOULD BRING HIM INTO
SO HE STARED AT THE LIVING PERFECTION
OF THE COLORFUL SLIPSTREAM STILL
WANTING BUT THIS TIME SOAKING THE
SIGHTS INTO HIMSELF FOR HE WOULD NOT
REMEMBER IT ANYMORE WHEN THE MOMENT
CAME AND LIKE WHISPERS WOULD BE GONE

TICK TOCK

ROW UPON ROW LINED UP LIKE MARCHING
FLESH LAYING ON WHITE COFFIN BED
HUMANS HOOKED INTO INTRA VEIN NOT
WANTING TO LIVE THE LIFE OF PAIN
GLASS RED BOTTLES SAY THE NUMBERS
CLOCKS COUNTING BACKWARDS LIKE
BABY SCREAM STRAPPED INTO PLACE WITH
VELCRO OF NYLON THREAD WITH SICK
WHITE GLOW OF THE FLUORESENCE ABOVE
THIS PLACE DARK IMMENSE AND SANQUINE
IN DARK LIGHT BEATING THE HEARTS IN
ADDICTION TIME OF MATERIAL AND VAIN
HUNGER PANGS OF VIOLENT PAST AND
BLEEDING BRAINS THAT SURGE WITH
CHEMICAL BREATH IN HALF LIFE DRAIN
EMOTION LIVING WITH SHAKY FLATLINE
GRAY AND BRIGHT FLESH SKIN HANGS
TO CLUTCH LIFE UPON BONES THAT ACHE
THE NUMBERS READINGS ALWAYS DIFFER
FROM ONE TO NEXT AND NEVER THE SAME
FOR THERES ALWAYS TIME ALWAYS TIME
TIME NEVER TELLS YOU UNTIL ITS TOO LATE
TICK TOCK TICK TOCK THE CLOCK
THE CLOCK IS THE FLESH KILLER

INNOCENCE

DEEP WITHIN WET
GLOSSY PULSATING
INTERIOR OF THE EBONY
VULVA WAS INJECTED THE
SEED OF INNOCENCE THAT
WAS ALLOWED THE GIFT
TO ROAM AND BE FREE
TO METAMORPHOSE AND
GESTATE TO MATURITY
BUT NO ONE KNEW OF A
CANCER CELL LURKIUNG
INSIDE WITH IT – RAGE – IT
WAS JEALOUS OF ITS BEING
AND SPIRIT THAT IT ATTACKED
IT RAPING ITS PURITY AWAY
WHERE NOW INNOCENCE
WOULD BE REBIRTHED
PREMATURE FROM WOMB
TO UN – DIMENSION AFTER
CHRONOS THE BIRTH AS FLESH
REPLICATED FELL OUT
SHAKING AS CONFUSION

THE CRIMSON DISC
SETTING IN THE AFAR
SLEEPS IN SILENCE
AMONG WAVES OF
A SURGING SEA
WITH MY REGRET

STARS CRY
EVENING COMES
A HEAVY FEELING
PRESSES DOWN ON ME
RAINS SILENT FROM
THE TWINIGHT

THE KEEPSAKE
OF THIS LOVE
HIDDEN DEEPLY
FROM LIGHT
ITS ECHO
A DILUTED
SCREAM
THIS PAIN
A THOUSAND
TINY DEATHS
UNENDING

THE DRIFTING CLOUDS
SOARING ABOVE THE SEA
REMINDS ME DEEPLY
OF WHAT ONCE WAS
WHAT WILL BE AGAIN
AND WHAT WAS
NEVER TO LAST

I GAZE AT
STILL FALLING SNOW
ANXIETY REMAINS
THE SLOW FLAKES
I THINK OF THE PAST
MANY SNOWS
I HAVE SEEN IN MY LIFE
MY SOUL HAS
EVEN FORGOTTEN
PHOBIA REMAINS

THE TATTOO BURNS
OF MY FORBIDDEN LOVE
ITS BURN IS ALL TOO
FAMILIAR TO MEMORY
A SECRET FLEETING
THE WINDS OF SILENT STARS
THIS FORBIDDEN LOVE
WAS NEVER WRONG
ONLY MISUNDERSTOOD
TO A BREATH AND
BEATING HEART

AS
I BREATHE
I INHALE
YOUR KISSES
AND EXHALE
YOUR TONGUE
WHICH FILLS ME
WITH DEEP
LONGING
FOR YOU

SOARING THROUGH
THE SKY OF MIND
MY SOUL WAS SPLIT IN TWO
ONE PART OF ME WANTED
TO HOLD YOU IN MY ARMS
THE OTHER WISHED
I HAD NEVER MET YOU
CAUSE THIS EMPTINESS
I WOULD NEVER KNOW
AND STILL IM SPLIT IN TWO

I GAZE OUT
MY WINDOW
THE MEMORY
OF YOU INSIDE
RAIN AND ICE
COVER THE VIEW
UNTIL I CANNOT
SEE ANYONE
STILL THE
MEMORY
RESIDES

I EAT
CONSUMED
THE FLAMES OF SUN
A EUPHORIA
TRANSFIXED
IM TRAPPED LAPPING
UPON THE KISS
THIS LOVE
FOREVER
AND EVER
A WISH

TONIGHT
THE STARS
KNOW OF MY PAST
COLD FLAKES FALL
UPON THE SEA
DISAPPEARING
ONE BY ONE
I SIT GAZING
A WIND HOWLS
ROARING COLD
I HAVE YOUR LOVE
TO WARM MY SKIN
THIS NIGHT

SLEEP DOES NOT
COME TONIGHT
I SLEEP WITH
MY ANXIETY
I SHARE WITH
MY HEARTS FEARS
I AM NOT ALONE
IN THE SILENCE
OF THIS ROOM
AT LEAST I HAVE
MY ANXIETY
AS MY KEEPSAKE

MY HEARTS SONG
IS THE STAIN
YOU LEFT UPON IT
IT SOUNDS LIKE
MANY SORROWS
THE RAIN DROPS OUTSIDE
DO NOT BRING ME COMFORT
ONLY THE MEMORY OF YOU
DISTRACTS FROM
THE STAIN

TWINIGHT
MY THOUGHTS
DEEPEN
OF THE LOVE
I LET SLIP AWAY
ARE YOU LOVED
BY ANOTHER?
MY HEART DOES
NOT KNOW

MY MEMORIES
VANISH IN EMPTY SKY
WHITE FALL OUTSIDE
I LISTEN TO THE WIND
BUT ALL I HEAR
IS SILENCE

THE MEMORY
OF YOU
THIS SPLINTER
IN MY HEART
HOW CAN
SOMETHING
SO SMALL
CAUSE ONE
SO MUCH
GRIEF

MUSIC BY
ANGELO SPIZZARRI

RED HAZE
FUTURESHOCK
SOMNAMBULIST
MELTDOWN
GHOSTLIGHT

ALBUMS AVAILABLE
@ AMAZON, CdBaby
& iTUNES mP3 & CD

www.SPIZZARRI.com

FOR INFORMATION
ON MUSIC, BOOKS &
OTHER EVENTS
PLEASE VISIT THESE
WEBSITES BELOW:

WWW.SPIZZARRI.COM
FACEBOOK.COM/SPIZZARRI
INSTAGRAM.COM/SPIZZARRI
TWITTER.COM/SPIZZARRI

"REALITY IS ONES OWN PERCEPTION."

www.SPIZZARRI.com

www.ingramcontent.com/pod-product-compliance
Lightning Source LLC
Chambersburg PA
CBHW020658300426
44112CB00007B/431